Manual
of
PRAISE

Tools to Enter
the Presence of God

By Brendan Case

www.BrendanCase.com

A City of the Lord Publication

Phoenix · Los Angeles · San Diego · Monterey Bay

D1444422

Publisher: City of the Lord
                     711 W University Drive
                     Tempe, Arizona 85281
                     480-968-5895
                     www.cityofthelord.org
                     PhoenixBranch@cityofthelord.org

City of the Lord is officially established as a Private
Association of the Christian Faithful and Private Juridic
Person of Diocesan Right by Bishop Thomas J. Omsted,
May 8, 2012. City of the Lord is also a founding member of
the Catholic Fraternity, a private association of the
Catholic faithful, established in the Vatican by Pope Saint
John Paul II on November 30, 1990.

Printed in the United States of America.
Manual of PRAISE
Written by Brendan Case
Cover art by Brendan Case

ISBN -- 13-978-0-9915327-2-8

Table of Contents

3

4

Introduction

One morning I awoke to enter into my time with the Lord
to find that my head was still asleep. It is my custom to
start my prayer time by praising Him as He rightly
deserves. I opened my mouth and nothing came out. I
tried and tried and apologized and apologized.
I don't know if you ever have experiences like this, but...
I needed a practical tool, not only for when my head was
dead, but also for the times when I am facing a dry season.
It is out of my simple experience of my human need that I
wrote this little prayer book, Manual of PRAISE. I pray that
it is a tool to help you enter His presence and encounter
the One who longs to encounter you.

With all the love in my heart
I am your little brother in Jesus,
Brendan, son of the Father

How to Use this Prayer Book

1. Acknowledge the Presence (Matthew 1:23)

Stop. Slow down. Begin your prayer time by acknowledging the presence of God who has been waiting for you. This is a time of encounter, of being with. Many times we approach prayer as a task, rather than a relationship. Prayer is not what you do. Prayer is who you are with. Be with the Father. Be with Jesus. Be with the Holy Spirit. Prayer takes great intention and attention.

2. Declare Your Dependency (Romans 8:26)

Prayer is not something we can do. It is the work of the Holy Spirit in us. We need the Holy Spirit to be able to pray. He is the one that cries out, in us, "Abba, Father!" Our place is to become aware of that cry and let him do it through us.

3. Surrender to Praise (Psalm 34:1)

Begin to thumb though the first half of the book and start reciting to God the different phrases, titles and adjectives as you read. Open your mouth and speak His praise. Scripture is clear that we are to

Through Jesus, therefore, let us continually offer to God a sacrifice of praise—the fruit of lips that openly profess his name. Hebrews 13:15

Sample Prayer:

Father,
you are here and have been waiting for me.
It is You that longs for me.
It is You that thirst for me.
Holy Spirit,
you are my Helper.
I cannot pray as I ought.

Please come and help me.
I surrender this time to the Lordship of Jesus.
Jesus, have your way.
Father,
In Jesus name I pray.
AMEN

4. Enter into the Word of God

POPE FRANCIS on Praise

MORNING MEDITATION IN THE CHAPEL OF THE *DOMUS SANCTAE MARTHAE*
The prayer of praise - Tuesday, 28 January 2014
(by *L'Osservatore Romano*, Weekly ed. in English, n. 5, 31 January 2014)

Pope Francis continued his reflection on the second Book of Samuel (6:12-15, 17-17) which tells of David's dancing before the Ark of the Lord on its entry into Jerusalem. "King David," the Pope said, "offered sacrifice in honor of God; he prayed. Then his prayer became exultant ... it became the prayer of praise and of joy, and he began to dance. The Bible says: 'David danced before the Lord with all his might'", and he rejoiced greatly as he offers praise to the Lord. "That," Pope Francis said, "was truly the prayer of praise".

Pope Francis remarked: "I thought immediately of Sarah after she gave birth to Isaac: 'God has made laughter for me; everyone who hears will laugh over me'. This elderly woman at the age of 90 laughed and danced for joy". David was young, but he also "danced, he danced before the Lord. This is an example of the prayer of praise".

The prayer of praise is quite different than the prayer we normally raise to God, the Pope continued, when "we ask something of the Lord" or even "thank the Lord". "We often leave aside the prayer of praise". It doesn't come so easily to us, he said. Some might think that this kind of prayer is only "for those who belong to the renewal in the spirit movement, not for all Christians. The prayer of praise is a Christian prayer for all of us. Each day during Mass, when we sing: 'Holy, Holy...', this is the prayer of praise. We praise God for his greatness, for he is great. And we tell him beautiful things, because we like it to be so". And it does not matter if we are good singers, the Pope remarked. In fact, he said, it is impossible to imagine that "you are able to shout out when your team scores a goal and you cannot sing the Lord's praises, and leave behind your composure a little to sing".

Praising God is "totally gratuitous", Pope Francis continued. "We do not ask; we do not thank. We praise: you are great. 'Glory be to the Father, and to the Son, and to the Holy Spirit...'. We say this with all our heart. It is also an act of justice, for he is great, he is our God. Let us think about a good question we can ask ourselves today: How is my prayer of praise? Do I know how to praise the Lord? Or when I pray the *Gloria* or the *Sanctus*, do I only pray with my lips and not with all my heart? What does David's dancing say to me? And Sarah who dances for joy? As David enters into the city, he begins something else as well: celebration. The joy of praise leads us to the joy of celebration". This celebration then extends to the whole family, the Pope continued. "Each person was given a cake of bread and departed to his own house to celebrate" (cf. v. 19). But when David reentered his household, he had to face the reproach and scorn of Michal, the daughter of

King Saul: "'Aren't you ashamed of what you have done? How could you have done this, you the king, dancing in front of everyone? Are you not ashamed?" I wonder how many times in our hearts we hold in contempt good people who praise the Lord, so spontaneously, as it comes to them.

In the Bible, the Pope recalled, we read that "'Michal had no child to the day of her death'. What does the word of God mean here? That joy that the prayer of praise makes us fruitful. Sarah was dancing for joy at 90 years old in the great moment of her fruitfulness! Fruitfulness gives praise to the Lord". The man or woman who praises the Lord, who prays by praising the Lord and rejoice "as they sing the *Sanctus* at Mass" is fruitful. On the other hand, the Pope said, those who "close themselves into the formality of a cold, measured prayer perhaps end up like Michal, in the sterility of formality".

"Let us think of and imagine David who dances with all his might before the Lord. Let us think about how beautiful it is to offer the prayer of praise. Perhaps it will do us good to repeat the words of the psalm we just prayed, number 24: 'Lift up your heads, O gates! And be lifted up, O ancient doors! That the King of glory may come in, the Lord strong and mighty, he is the king of glory! Lift up your heads O gates! Who is this king of glory? The Lord of hosts, he is the king of glory!'". This ought to be our prayer of praise, Pope Francis said. And he concluded: when we raise this prayer to the Lord we ought "to say to our heart: 'Lift up your hearts, for you stand before the king of glory'".

Praise Phrases

Alleluia

Awesome are You

Be Blessed, O God

Be Exalted, O God

Be Magnified, O God

Blessed be God

Blessed be the Father, the Son, and the Holy Spirit

You are All Knowing *(Omniscient)*

You are All Powerful *(Omnipotent)*

You are All Present

You are All Wise

You are Eternal

You are Existence

You are All Good

You are All Gracious

You are Holy

Blessed be His Holy Name

Blessed be His Most Precious Blood

Blessed be the Name of Jesus

Blessed be the Sacred Heart of Jesus

Blessed be Your Name

Glory, Honor, and Praise to You

Glory to God in the Highest Glory to You

Great are You

Holy are You

Holy, Holy, Holy Lord

Holy, Holy, Holy is the Lord, Who Was, Who is and Who is to come

I bless You
I exalt You
I glorify You
I honor You
I Love You
Jesus
Praise You
Jesus Lover of Mankind
Mighty are You
My All and All
My Lord and My God
My Lord and My God
My King and My All
There is No Other
You are Vanquisher of Hell
We Give You Thanks
We Worship
Worthy are You
You are Great, You are Holy
You are My God, You are My king
You are Seated at the Right Hand of the Father
You are the Name Above All Names
You are the Resurrected One
You Take Away the Sins of the World
Worthy are You
You are Immutable *(Unchanging)*
You Incomprehensible
Infinite All Just Life Love Judge
You are All Merciful
Personal

You are Self-existent
You are Self-sufficient
You are Sovereign
You are the Supreme Being
You are Transcendent

Your Favorite Praise Phrases:

Titles for God

Most Holy Trinity
Three Divine Persons
The One in Three and the Three in One
Ancient of Days (Daniel 7:9)
Arm of the Lord (Isaiah 53:1)
Battle Bow (Zechariah 10:4
Branch (Zechariah 6:12)
Consuming Fire (Deuteronomy 4:24)
Covenant to the People (Isaiah 42:6)
Creator (Ecclesiastes 12:1)
Creator of Israel (Isaiah 43:15)
Crown of Glory and Diadem (Isaiah 28:5)
God my Exceeding Joy (Psalm 43:4)
God of My Right (Psalm 4:1)
God of My Salvation (Psalm 18:46)
God of the Whole Earth (Isaiah 54:5)
Husband (Isaiah 54:5)
King (Isaiah 6:5)
King of Glory (Psalm 24:7)
Lifter of My Head (Psalm 3:3)
Light of Israel (Isaiah 10:17)
Lord of the Whole Earth (Micah 4:13)
Messenger of The Covenant (Malachi 3:1)
Messiah the Prince (Daniel 9:25)
My Chosen Portion (Psalm 16:5)
My Cup (Psalm 16:5)
My Deliver (Psalm 40:17)
My Father (Psalm 89:26)

My Fortress (Psalm 31:3)
My Glory (Psalm 3:3)
My God (Psalm 3:7)
My Help (Psalm 22:19)
My Hiding Place (Psalm 32:7)
My Hope (Psalm 71:5)
My King (Psalm 5:2)
My Light (Psalm 27:1)
My Portion (Psalm 119:57)
My Portion in the Land of the Living (Psalm 142:5)
My Redeemer (Psalm 19:14)
My Refuge (Psalm 46:1)
My Rock (Psalm 19:14)
My Shield (Psalm 28:7)
My Shepherd (Psalm 23:1)
My Song (Psalm 118:14)
My Strength (Psalm 18:1)
My Stronghold (Psalm 18:2)
My Strong Refuge (Psalm 71:7)
My Strong Deliverer (Psalm 140:7)
Potter (Isaiah 64:8)
Redeemer of Israel (Isaiah 49:7)
Rock of my Strength (Psalm 62:7)
Rock of Israel (2 Samuel 23:3)
Ruler of Israel (Micah 5:2)
Savior (Isaiah 45:15)
Shepherd (Genesis 49:24)
Shepherd of Israel (Psalm 80:1)
Shiloh (Genesis 49:10)
Star (Numbers 24:17)

Stone (Psalm 118:22)
Stone of Israel (Genesis 49:24)
Stronghold of my Life (Psalm 27:1)
The King of Israel (Zephaniah 3:15)
Upholder of My Life (Psalm 54:4)
Upright One (Isaiah 26:7)

Hebrew Names of God

Adon – Lord (Joshua 3:11)

Adonai—Lord (Genesis 15:2)

Ha Shem - The Name (Leviticus 24:16)

The God of Abraham, Isaac, and Jacob (Exodus 3:15)

The Great, Mighty, Awesome God (Deuteronomy 10:17)

The El Names of God

Elohim—The Creator (Genesis 1:1)

El Elyon - The Most High (Genesis 14:18-20)

El Shaddai - The Almighty Who is Able to Do as He has
Promised (Genesis 17:1-2)

El Chaseddi - The God of Mercy (Psalm 59:10)

El Emanuh - The Faithful Go (Deuteronomy 7:9)

El Kanna - The Jealous God (Exodus 20:5)

Elohe Tishuath - God of My Salvation (Psalm 51:14)

El Olam - Everlasting God (Genesis 21:33)

Elohim Kadesh - God the Holy One (Habakkuk 1:12)

M'kaddesh El Israel - Holy One of Israel (Psalm 68:35)

The Yahweh/Jehovah names of God

Yahweh/Jehovah – God (Exodus 6:3)

Eheyeh asher Eheyah - I am Who Am (Exodus 3:14)

Yahweh Yireh—God who Sees and Provides (Genesis
22:14)

Yahweh Sabaoth - God of Armies (1 Samuel 1:3)

Yahweh Rapha - God my Healer (Exodus 15:26)

Yahweh Nissi - God my Banner (Exodus 17:15)

Yahweh M'kaddesh - God Who Sanctifies (Exodus 31:13)

Yahweh Shalom - God who is Peace (Judges 6:24)

Yahweh Roe - God who is Shepherd (Psalm 23:1)

Yahweh Hoseenu - God who is Creator (Psalm 95:6)

Yahweh Tsidkenu - God who is Righteous (Jeremiah 23:6)

Yahweh Shammah - God who is Present/Available
(Ezekiel 48:35)

Yahweh Gibbor Michamah - The Lord Mighty in Battle
(Psalm 24:8)

Yahweh Makkeh - The Lord that Smiteth (Ezekiel 7:9)

Yahweh Chereb - The Lord, the Sword (Deuteronomy
33:29)

Yahweh Maginennu - The Lord our Defense (Psalm 80:18)

Yahweh Magen - The Lord, the Shield (Deuteronomy
33:29)

Hamelekh Hagoel - Redeeming Angel (Genesis 48:16)

Peleh Yo'etz - Wonderful Counselor (Isaiah 9:6)

Sar Shalom - Prince of Peace (Isaiah 9:6)

Tsur Yeshuato - Rock of His Salvation (Deuteronomy 32:15)

Names of the Father

Abba (Romans 8:15)
Father (Matthew 6:9)
Father of Our Lord Jesus Christ (Colossians 1:3)
Father of Glory (Ephesians 1:17)
Father of Lights (James 1:17)
Father of Mercies (2 Corinthians 1:3)
Father of Spirits (Hebrews 12:9)
God of All Comfort (2 Corinthians 1:3)
God of Peace (Hebrews 13:20)
God the Father (2 Timothy 1:2)
Immortal (1 Timothy 1:17)
Invisible (1 Timothy 1:7)
King of the Ages (Revelations 15:4)
Majestic Glory (2 Peter 1:17)
My Father (Matthew 7:21)
Only God (1 Timothy 1:17)
Power (Mark 14:62)
The Almighty (Revelations 1:8)
The Creator (Romans 1:25)
The God of Glory (Acts 7:2)
The God of Our Fathers (Acts 7:32)
The Law Giver and Judge (James 4:12)
The Living God (2 Corinthians 6:16)
The Lord God of Israel (Luke 2:68)
The Majesty (Hebrews 1:3)
The Vine Dresser (John 15:1)
Your Father (Matthew 5:45)

Names of Jesus

Author of Life (Acts 3:15)
Advocate (1 John 2:1)
Beloved Son (Matthew 3:17)
Chief Shepherd (1 Peter 5:4)
Faithful Witness (Revelations 1:5)
Firstborn (Hebrews 1:6)
Firstborn of All Creation (Colossians 1:15)
First from the Dead (Revelations 1:5)
God's Mystery (Colossians 2:2)
Good Shepherd (John 10:11)
Great High Priest (Hebrews 4:14)
Head Over All Things (Ephesians 1:22)
Heir of All Things (Hebrews 1:2)
Holy One (Acts 3:14)
Holy Servant (Acts 4:27)
Horn of Salvation (Luke 1:69)
I AM (John 8:58)
Immanuel (Matthew 1:23)
Light of the World (John 8:12)
Jesus (Matthew 1:21)
Jesus of Nazareth (Matthew 26:71)
Judge of the Living and the Dead (Acts 10:42)
King of Israel (Mark 15:32)
King of Jews (Matthew 27:37)
King of Kings and Lord of Lords (Revelations 1916)
Lamb of God (John 1:36)
Lion of Judah (Revelations 5:5)
Lord and Teacher (John 13:14)

Master (Luke 8:24)

Mediator (1 Timothy 2:5)

My Beloved (Matthew 12:18)

Mighty God (Isaiah 9:6)

Only Begotten Son (1 John 4:9)

Paschal Lamb (1 Corinthians 5:7)

Pioneer and Perfector of Our Faith (Hebrews 12:2)

Prince (Acts 5:31)

Prince of Peace (Isaiah 9:6)

Righteous One (Acts 3:14)

Root and Offspring of David (Revelations 22:16)

Savior of All Men (1 Timothy 4:10)

Savior of the World (John 4:42)

Shepherd and Guardian of Our Souls (1 Peter 2:25)

Son of David (Matthew 1:1)

Son of Abraham (Matthew 1:1)

Son of Joseph (Matthew 1:20)

Son of Man (Matthew 26:64)

Son of the Father (2 John 1:3)

Son of the Most High (Luke 1:32)

Stone (Mark 12:10)

The Alpha and Omega (Revelations 22:13)

The Amen (Revelations 3:14)

The Apostle (Hebrews 3:1)

The Beginning and the End (Revelation 22:13)

The Bread of God (John 6:33)

The Bread of Life (John 6:35)

The Bridegroom (John 3:29)

The Bright Morning Star (Revelations 22:16)

The Chosen One (Luke 9:35)

The Deliver (Romans 11:26)
The Door (John 10:7)
The Expected One (Luke 7:19)
The Faithful and True One (Revelations 19:11)
The First and the Last (Revelations 22:13)
The Head of the Body, the Church (Colossians 1:18)
The Image of the Invisible God (Colossians 1:15)
The Lamb (Revelations 5:12)
The Last Adam (1 Corinthians 15:45)
The Man (John 19:5)
The Messiah (John 1:41)
The Power of God (1 Corinthians 1:24)
The Prophet (John 1:25)
The Resurrection (John 11:25)
The Son of God (Matthew 26:63)
The True Bread from Heaven (John 6:32)
The True Vine (John 15:1)
The Way, the Truth, and the Life (John 14:6)
The Wisdom of God (1 Corinthians 1:24)
The Word (John 1:1)
The Word of God (Revelations 19:13)
The Word of Life (1 John 1:1)
Wonderful Counselor (Isaiah 9:6)

Names of the Holy Spirit

The Holy Spirit (Luke 3:16)
Spirit of God (Romans 8:9)
The Holy Spirit of God (Ephesians 4:30)
Breath of Life from God (Revelations 11:11)
Breath of the Lord (Isaiah 40:7)
Counselor (John 14:26)
Finger of God (Luke 11:20)
Fullness of God (Ephesians 3:19)
Gift of God (John 4:10)
God's Blessing (Isaiah 44:3)
God's Good Spirit (Nehemiah 9:20)
Oil of Gladness (Ps 45:7)
Lord Who is the Spirit (2 Corinthians 3:18)
Spring of Water (John 4:14)
Spirit of Adoption (Romans 8:15)
Spirit of Burning (Isaiah 4:4)
Spirit of Christ (Romans 8:9)
Spirit of Compassion (Zechariah 12:10)
Spirit of Glory (1 Peter 4:14)
Spirit of Him Who Raised Jesus from the Dead (Romans 8:11)
Spirit of Holiness (Romans 1:4)
Spirit of Life in Christ Jesus (Romans 8:2)
Spirit of Power (2 Timothy 1:7)
Spirit of Prophecy (Revelations 1:10)
Spirit of Love (2 Timothy 1:7)
Spirit of Revelation (Ephesians 1:17)
Spirit of Self-Control (2 Timothy 1:7)

Spirit of Supplication (Zechariah 12:10)
Spirit of Truth (John 14:17)
Spirit of Witness (Hebrews 10:15)
The Anointing (1 John 2:27)
The Breath of God's Nostrils (Psalm 18:15)
The Breath of the Almighty (Job 33:4)
The Eternal Spirit (Hebrews 9:14)
The Hand of God (2 Chronicles 30:12)
The Hand of the Lord (Isaiah 41:20)
The Holy Spirit Sent from Heaven (1 Peter 1:12)
The Holy Spirit Who Dwells Within Us (1 Timothy 1:14)
The Holy Spirit Within Me (1 Corinthians 6:19)
The Power of the Most High (Luke 1:35)
The Promise (Acts 2:39)
The Promise of the Father (Luke 24:49)
The Promised Holy Spirit (Ephesians 1:13)
The Spirit (Romans 2:29)
The Spirit of Christ (Romans 8:9)
The Spirit of Jesus (Acts 16:7)
The Spirit of Jesus Christ (Philippians 16:7)
The Spirit of the Living God (2 Corinthians 3:3)
Water on the Thirsty Land (Isaiah 44:3)

Adjectives for Praising

Able
Absorbing
Abundant
Accurate
Adventurous
Affirmative
Alluring
Amazing
Ample
Ancient
Appealing
Artistic
Astonishing
Astounding
Attentive
Attractive
Audacious
Awe-inspiring
Awesome
Beautiful
Best
Beyond Belief
Big
Bold
Booming
Bottomless
Bountiful
Brainy

Brave
Brawny
Bright
Brilliant
Bubbly
Calming
Captivating
Caring
Careful
Champion
Cheerful
Cheery
Classy
Clear
Clever
Close
Coach
Comforting
Compassionate
Complex
Concerned
Considerate
Cool
Copious
Consoling
Courageous
Courteous
Cozy

Creative	Fathomless
Daring	Faultless
Dazzling	Fearless
Deep	Fierce
Defending	Fine
Delightful	Firm
Desirable	Flawless
Determined	Flourishing
Dignified	Fond
Distinctive	Forbearing
Ecstatic	Forgiving
Elating	Frank
Electrifying	Fresh
Empathetic	Friendly
Endowed	Full
Endless	Full of Life
Engrossing	Gallant
Enlivening	Generous
Enormous	Gentle
Enthralling	Genuine
Exceptional	Gifted
Exciting	Gigantic
Exhilarating	Gleaming
Expansive	Glorious
Expert	Good
Extraordinary	Gorgeous
Extreme	Gracious
Fabulous	Grand
Fair	Great
Fascinating	Gregarious

Grisly
Gushy
Handsome
Handy
Happy
Health
Hefty
Helpful
Holy
Homey
Huge
Humble
Immaculate
Imperial
Incomparable
Inconceivable
Incredible
Indestructible
Indomitable
Inestimable
Infinite
Ingenious
Invincible
Illuminating
Immeasurable
Instructive
Intense
Interesting
Invaluable
Inventive

Invigorating
Jolly
Jovial
Joyful
Keen
Kind
Kindhearted
Kingly
Knowledgeable
Lacking Nothing
Large
Lavish
Light
Listener
Lively
Lofty
Loud
Lovely
Loving
Loyal
Luminous
Magnanimous
Magnificent
Majestic
Marvelous
Matchless
Meek
Merciful
Merry
Mighty

Mild	Prosperous
Miraculous	Protective
Most	Pure
Multifaceted	Quiet
Mysterious	Radical
Navigator	Radiant
Near	Rapturous
New	Rare
Noble	Ready
Nourishing	Reassuring
Optimistic	Regal
Original	Remarkable
Outstanding	Remissive
Overwhelming	Resolute
Pardoning	Resourceful
Patient	Respectful
Peaceful	Rich
Perfect	Righteous
Pleasant	Riveting
Plentiful	Rousing
Polite	Safe
Positive	Sane
Powerful	Selfless
Precious	Sharp
Pretty	Shielding
Priceless	Shinning
Proficient	Simple
Profound	Smart
Profuse	Soft
Promising	Soothing

Sound
Sparkling
Specific
Spectacular
Spicy
Splendid
Spotless
Spry
Spunky
Stately
Stern
Still
Stimulating
Stupendous
Straight
Strong
Sturdy
Successful
Sunny
Supportive
Sure
Sweet
Sympathetic
Talented
Terrific
Thoughtful
Thought-Provoking
Thriving
Triumphant
Too much

Trainer
True
Trustworthy
Unassailable
Unbeatable
Unblemished
Unbound
Unconquerable
Unfathomable
Unique
Unlimited
Unquestionable
Unrepressed
Unrestrained
Unrivaled
Unshakable
Unsullied
Unsurpassed
Untamed
Untarnished
Unusual
Upbeat
Valiant
Vanquisher
Vast
Venerable
Vicious
Victor
Vivacious
Vivid

Warm
Weighty
Welcoming
Wide
Wild
Wise
Everything I ever dreamed

Without Doubt
Without Equal
Witty
Wonderful
Wondrous
Worthy

Psalms of Praise and Thanksgiving

The psalms are the ancient prayer book of Israel. Many are attributed to King David, the shepherd boy, who wrote and sang them to the Shepherd of Israel as he sat in the wild, alone with the Alone. As the years passed these prayers were used in the Temple liturgy as the prescribed morning and evening sacrifices were offered to Yahweh.

Since the beginning of the New Israel, the Church, these same psalms have served as the central prayer book of worship. Seven times a day, monks stop, pray and then return to their work, sanctifying their day by praying the Word of God, centering their calendar on the heavenly worship of Jesus, the Great High Priest. This prayer is called the Liturgy of the Hours. You can buy many versions of the Hours and can also download apps. I recommend this, if you do not have the Liturgy of the Hours.

Take these prayers and make them your own.

Read them out loud.

Read them with the drama that makes them your own, with the intonation of your heart.

Read them, stop and let rise from your heart.

It is usual to end the praying of the psalm with:

+Glory to the Father, and to the Son, and to the Holy. As it was in the beginning, is now and will be forever.

Psalm 100

[1] Shout for joy to the LORD, all the earth.
[2] Worship the LORD with gladness;
   come before him with joyful songs.
[3] Know that the LORD is God.
   It is he who made us, and we are his;
   we are his people, the sheep of his pasture.
[4] Enter his gates with thanksgiving
   and his courts with praise;
   give thanks to him and praise his name.
[5] For the LORD is good and his love endures forever;
   his faithfulness continues through all generations.

Psalm 95

[1] Come, let us sing for joy to the LORD;
   let us shout aloud to the Rock of our salvation.
[2] Let us come before him with thanksgiving
   and extol him with music and song.
[3] For the LORD is the great God,
   the great King above all gods.
[4] In his hand are the depths of the earth,
   and the mountain peaks belong to him.
[5] The sea is his, for he made it,
   and his hands formed the dry land.
[6] Come, let us bow down in worship,

let us kneel before the LORD our Maker;
7 for he is our God and we are the people of his pasture,
  the flock under his care.
  Today, if only you would hear his voice,
8 "Do not harden your hearts as you did at Meribah,
  as you did that day at Massah in the wilderness,
9 where your ancestors tested me;
  they tried me, though they had seen what I did.
10 For forty years I was angry with that generation;
  I said, 'They are a people whose hearts go astray,
  and they have not known my ways.'
11 So I declared on oath in my anger,
  'They shall never enter my rest.'"

Psalm 96

1 Sing to the LORD a new song;
  sing to the LORD, all the earth.
2 Sing to the LORD, praise his name;
  proclaim his salvation day after day.
3 Declare his glory among the nations,
  his marvelous deeds among all peoples.

4 For great is the LORD and most worthy of praise;
  he is to be feared above all gods.
5 For all the gods of the nations are idols,
  but the LORD made the heavens.
6 Splendor and majesty are before him;
  strength and glory are in his sanctuary.

⁷ Ascribe to the Lord, all you families of nations,
  ascribe to the Lord glory and strength.
⁸ Ascribe to the Lord the glory due his name;
  bring an offering and come into his courts.
⁹ Worship the Lord in the splendor of his holiness;
  tremble before him, all the earth.
¹⁰ Say among the nations, "The Lord reigns."
  The world is firmly established, it cannot be moved;
  he will judge the peoples with equity.

¹¹ Let the heavens rejoice, let the earth be glad;
  let the sea resound, and all that is in it.
¹² Let the fields be jubilant, and everything in them;
  let all the trees of the forest sing for joy.
¹³ Let all creation rejoice before the Lord, for he comes,
  he comes to judge the earth.
He will judge the world in righteousness
  and the peoples in his faithfulness.

Psalm 92

¹ It is good to praise the Lord
  and make music to your name, O Most High,
² proclaiming your love in the morning
  and your faithfulness at night,
³ to the music of the ten-stringed lyre
  and the melody of the harp.

⁴ For you make me glad by your deeds, Lord;
  I sing for joy at what your hands have done.
⁵ How great are your works, Lord,

how profound your thoughts!
⁶Senseless people do not know,
  fools do not understand,
⁷that though the wicked spring up like grass
  and all evildoers flourish,
  they will be destroyed forever.

⁸But you, LORD, are forever exalted.

⁹For surely your enemies, LORD,
  surely your enemies will perish;
  all evildoers will be scattered.
¹⁰You have exalted my horn like that of a wild ox;
  fine oils have been poured on me.
¹¹My eyes have seen the defeat of my adversaries;
  my ears have heard the rout of my wicked foes.

¹²The righteous will flourish like a palm tree,
  they will grow like a cedar of Lebanon;
¹³planted in the house of the LORD,
  they will flourish in the courts of our God.
¹⁴They will still bear fruit in old age,
  they will stay fresh and green,
¹⁵proclaiming, "The LORD is upright;
  he is my Rock, and there is no wickedness in him."

Psalm 97

¹The LORD reigns, let the earth be glad;
  let the distant shores rejoice.
²Clouds and thick darkness surround him;

righteousness and justice are the foundation of his throne.
³ Fire goes before him
and consumes his foes on every side.
⁴ His lightning lights up the world;
the earth sees and trembles.
⁵ The mountains melt like wax before the LORD,
before the Lord of all the earth.
⁶ The heavens proclaim his righteousness,
and all peoples see his glory.

⁷ All who worship images are put to shame,
those who boast in idols—
worship him, all you gods!

⁸ Zion hears and rejoices
and the villages of Judah are glad
because of your judgments, LORD.
⁹ For you, LORD, are the Most High over all the earth;
you are exalted far above all gods.
¹⁰ Let those who love the LORD hate evil,
for he guards the lives of his faithful ones
and delivers them from the hand of the wicked.
¹¹ Light shines on the righteous
and joy on the upright in heart.
¹² Rejoice in the LORD, you who are righteous,
and praise his holy name.

Psalm 98

¹ Sing to the LORD a new song,

for he has done marvelous things;
his right hand and his holy arm
    have worked salvation for him.
2 The LORD has made his salvation known
    and revealed his righteousness to the nations.
3 He has remembered his love
    and his faithfulness to Israel;
all the ends of the earth have seen
    the salvation of our God.

4 Shout for joy to the LORD, all the earth,
    burst into jubilant song with music;
5 make music to the LORD with the harp,
    with the harp and the sound of singing,
6 with trumpets and the blast of the ram's horn—
    shout for joy before the LORD, the King.

7 Let the sea resound, and everything in it,
    the world, and all who live in it.
8 Let the rivers clap their hands,
    let the mountains sing together for joy;
9 let them sing before the LORD,
    for he comes to judge the earth.
He will judge the world in righteousness
    and the peoples with equity.

Psalm 110

1 The LORD says to my lord:

"Sit at my right hand

until I make your enemies
a footstool for your feet."

² The LORD will extend your mighty scepter from
Zion, saying,
  "Rule in the midst of your enemies!"
³ Your troops will be willing
  on your day of battle.
Arrayed in holy splendor,
  your young men will come to you
  like dew from the morning's womb.

⁴ The LORD has sworn
  and will not change his mind:
"You are a priest forever,
  in the order of Melchizedek."

⁵ The Lord is at your right hand;
  he will crush kings on the day of his wrath.
⁶ He will judge the nations, heaping up the dead
  and crushing the rulers of the whole earth.
⁷ He will drink from a brook along the way,
  and so he will lift his head high.

Psalm 111

¹ Praise the LORD.

I will extol the LORD with all my heart
  in the council of the upright and in the assembly.

² Great are the works of the LORD;
　　they are pondered by all who delight in them.
³ Glorious and majestic are his deeds,
　　and his righteousness endures forever.
⁴ He has caused his wonders to be remembered;
　　the LORD is gracious and compassionate.
⁵ He provides food for those who fear him;
　　he remembers his covenant forever.

⁶ He has shown his people the power of his works,
　　giving them the lands of other nations.
⁷ The works of his hands are faithful and just;
　　all his precepts are trustworthy.
⁸ They are established for ever and ever,
　　enacted in faithfulness and uprightness.
⁹ He provided redemption for his people;
　　he ordained his covenant forever—
　　holy and awesome is his name.

¹⁰ The fear of the LORD is the beginning of wisdom;
　　all who follow his precepts have good understanding.
　　To him belongs eternal praise.

Psalm 8

¹ LORD, our Lord,
　　how majestic is your name in all the earth!

You have set your glory
　　in the heavens.
² Through the praise of children and infants

you have established a stronghold against your enemies,
to silence the foe and the avenger.
³ When I consider your heavens,
the work of your fingers,
the moon and the stars,
which you have set in place,
⁴ what is mankind that you are mindful of them,
human beings that you care for them?

⁵ You have made them a little lower than the angels
and crowned them with glory and honor.
⁶ You made them rulers over the works of your hands;
you put everything under their feet:
⁷ all flocks and herds,
and the animals of the wild,
⁸ the birds in the sky,
and the fish in the sea,
all that swim the paths of the seas.

⁹ Lord, our Lord,
how majestic is your name in all the earth!

Psalm 134

¹ Praise the Lord, all you servants of the Lord
who minister by night in the house of the Lord.
² Lift up your hands in the sanctuary
and praise the Lord.

³ May the Lord bless you from Zion,
he who is the Maker of heaven and earth.

Psalm 135

¹ Praise the LORD.

Praise the name of the LORD;
    praise him, you servants of the LORD,
² you who minister in the house of the LORD,
    in the courts of the house of our God.

³ Praise the LORD, for the LORD is good;
    sing praise to his name, for that is pleasant.
⁴ For the LORD has chosen Jacob to be his own,
    Israel to be his treasured possession.

⁵ I know that the LORD is great,
    that our Lord is greater than all gods.
⁶ The LORD does whatever pleases him,
    in the heavens and on the earth,
    in the seas and all their depths.
⁷ He makes clouds rise from the ends of the earth;
    he sends lightning with the rain
    and brings out the wind from his storehouses.

⁸ He struck down the firstborn of Egypt,
    the firstborn of people and animals.
⁹ He sent his signs and wonders into your midst, Egypt,
    against Pharaoh and all his servants.
¹⁰ He struck down many nations
    and killed mighty kings—
¹¹ Sihon king of the Amorites,
    Og king of Bashan,

and all the kings of Canaan—
¹² and he gave their land as an inheritance,
an inheritance to his people Israel.

¹³ Your name, LORD, endures forever,
your renown, LORD, through all generations.
¹⁴ For the LORD will vindicate his people
and have compassion on his servants.

¹⁵ The idols of the nations are silver and gold,
made by human hands.
¹⁶ They have mouths, but cannot speak,
eyes, but cannot see.
¹⁷ They have ears, but cannot hear,
nor is there breath in their mouths.
¹⁸ Those who make them will be like them,
and so will all who trust in them.

¹⁹ All you Israelites, praise the LORD;
house of Aaron, praise the LORD;
²⁰ house of Levi, praise the LORD;
you who fear him, praise the LORD.
²¹ Praise be to the LORD from Zion,
to him who dwells in Jerusalem.

Praise the LORD.

Psalm 136

¹ Give thanks to the LORD, for he is good.

His love endures forever.
² Give thanks to the God of gods.
His love endures forever.
³ Give thanks to the Lord of lords:
His love endures forever.

⁴ to him who alone does great wonders,
His love endures forever.
⁵ who by his understanding made the heavens,
His love endures forever.
⁶ who spread out the earth upon the waters,
His love endures forever.
⁷ who made the great lights—
His love endures forever.
⁸ the sun to govern the day,
His love endures forever.
⁹ the moon and stars to govern the night;
His love endures forever.

¹⁰ to him who struck down the firstborn of Egypt
His love endures forever.
¹¹ and brought Israel out from among them
His love endures forever.
¹² with a mighty hand and outstretched arm;
His love endures forever.

¹³ to him who divided the Red Sea asunder
His love endures forever.
¹⁴ and brought Israel through the midst of it,
His love endures forever.
¹⁵ but swept Pharaoh and his army into the Red Sea;

His love endures forever.

¹⁶ to him who led his people through the wilderness;
His love endures forever.

¹⁷ to him who struck down great kings,
His love endures forever.
¹⁸ and killed mighty kings—
His love endures forever.
¹⁹ Sihon king of the Amorites
His love endures forever.
²⁰ and Og king of Bashan—
His love endures forever.
²¹ and gave their land as an inheritance,
His love endures forever.
²² an inheritance to his servant Israel.
His love endures forever.

²³ He remembered us in our low estate
His love endures forever.
²⁴ and freed us from our enemies.
His love endures forever.
²⁵ He gives food to every creature.
His love endures forever.

²⁶ Give thanks to the God of heaven.
His love endures forever.

Psalm 138

1 I will praise you, LORD, with all my heart;
   before the "gods" I will sing your praise.
2 I will bow down toward your holy temple
   and will praise your name
   for your unfailing love and your faithfulness,
for you have so exalted your solemn decree
   that it surpasses your fame.
3 When I called, you answered me;
   you greatly emboldened me.

4 May all the kings of the earth praise you, LORD,
   when they hear what you have decreed.
5 May they sing of the ways of the LORD,
   for the glory of the LORD is great.

6 Though the LORD is exalted, he looks kindly on the lowly;
   though lofty, he sees them from afar.
7 Though I walk in the midst of trouble,
   you preserve my life.
You stretch out your hand against the anger of my foes;
   with your right hand you save me.
8 The LORD will vindicate me;
   your love, LORD, endures forever—
   do not abandon the works of your hands.

Psalm 145

[1] I will exalt you, my God the King;
   I will praise your name for ever and ever.
[2] Every day I will praise you
   and extol your name for ever and ever.

[3] Great is the LORD and most worthy of praise;
   his greatness no one can fathom.
[4] One generation commends your works to another;
   they tell of your mighty acts.
[5] They speak of the glorious splendor of your majesty—
   and I will meditate on your wonderful works.
[6] They tell of the power of your awesome works—
   and I will proclaim your great deeds.
[7] They celebrate your abundant goodness
   and joyfully sing of your righteousness.

[8] The LORD is gracious and compassionate,
   slow to anger and rich in love.

[9] The LORD is good to all;
   he has compassion on all he has made.
[10] All your works praise you, LORD;
   your faithful people extol you.
[11] They tell of the glory of your kingdom
   and speak of your might,
[12] so that all people may know of your mighty acts
   and the glorious splendor of your kingdom.
[13] Your kingdom is an everlasting kingdom,
   and your dominion endures through all generations.

The LORD is trustworthy in all he promises
and faithful in all he does.
¹⁴ The LORD upholds all who fall
and lifts up all who are bowed down.
¹⁵ The eyes of all look to you,
and you give them their food at the proper time.
¹⁶ You open your hand
and satisfy the desires of every living thing.

¹⁷ The LORD is righteous in all his ways
and faithful in all he does.
¹⁸ The LORD is near to all who call on him,
to all who call on him in truth.
¹⁹ He fulfills the desires of those who fear him;
he hears their cry and saves them.
²⁰ The LORD watches over all who love him,
but all the wicked he will destroy.

²¹ My mouth will speak in praise of the LORD.
Let every creature praise his holy name
for ever and ever.

Psalm 146

¹ Praise the LORD. Praise the LORD, my soul.

² I will praise the LORD all my life;
I will sing praise to my God as long as I live.
³ Do not put your trust in princes,
in human beings, who cannot save.
⁴ When their spirit departs, they return to the ground;

on that very day their plans come to nothing.
⁵ Blessed are those whose help is the God of Jacob,
    whose hope is in the LORD their God.

⁶ He is the Maker of heaven and earth,
    the sea, and everything in them—
    he remains faithful forever.
⁷ He upholds the cause of the oppressed
    and gives food to the hungry.
The LORD sets prisoners free,
⁸   the LORD gives sight to the blind,
the LORD lifts up those who are bowed down,
    the LORD loves the righteous.
⁹ The LORD watches over the foreigner
    and sustains the fatherless and the widow,
    but he frustrates the ways of the wicked.

¹⁰ The LORD reigns forever,
    your God, O Zion, for all generations.

Praise the LORD.

Psalm 147

¹ Praise the LORD.

How good it is to sing praises to our God,
    how pleasant and fitting to praise him!

² The LORD builds up Jerusalem;

he gathers the exiles of Israel.
³ He heals the brokenhearted
   and binds up their wounds.
⁴ He determines the number of the stars
   and calls them each by name.
⁵ Great is our Lord and mighty in power;
   his understanding has no limit.
⁶ The LORD sustains the humble
   but casts the wicked to the ground.

⁷ Sing to the LORD with grateful praise;
   make music to our God on the harp.

⁸ He covers the sky with clouds;
   he supplies the earth with rain
   and makes grass grow on the hills.
⁹ He provides food for the cattle
   and for the young ravens when they call.

¹⁰ His pleasure is not in the strength of the horse,
   nor his delight in the legs of the warrior;
¹¹ the LORD delights in those who fear him,
   who put their hope in his unfailing love.

¹² Extol the LORD, Jerusalem;
   praise your God, Zion.

¹³ He strengthens the bars of your gates
   and blesses your people within you.
¹⁴ He grants peace to your borders
   and satisfies you with the finest of wheat.

¹⁵ He sends his command to the earth;
   his word runs swiftly.
¹⁶ He spreads the snow like wool
   and scatters the frost like ashes.
¹⁷ He hurls down his hail like pebbles.
   Who can withstand his icy blast?
¹⁸ He sends his word and melts them;
   he stirs up his breezes, and the waters flow.

¹⁹ He has revealed his word to Jacob,
   his laws and decrees to Israel.
²⁰ He has done this for no other nation;
   they do not know his laws.

Praise the LORD.

Psalm 148

¹ Praise the LORD.

Praise the LORD from the heavens;
   praise him in the heights above.
² Praise him, all his angels;
   praise him, all his heavenly hosts.
³ Praise him, sun and moon;
   praise him, all you shining stars.
⁴ Praise him, you highest heavens
   and you waters above the skies.

⁵ Let them praise the name of the LORD,

for at his command they were created,
⁶ and he established them for ever and ever—
   he issued a decree that will never pass away.

⁷ Praise the LORD from the earth,
   you great sea creatures and all ocean depths,
⁸ lightning and hail, snow and clouds,
   stormy winds that do his bidding,
⁹ you mountains and all hills,
   fruit trees and all cedars,
¹⁰ wild animals and all cattle,
   small creatures and flying birds,
¹¹ kings of the earth and all nations,
   you princes and all rulers on earth,
¹² young men and women,
   old men and children.

¹³ Let them praise the name of the LORD,
   for his name alone is exalted;
   his splendor is above the earth and the heavens.
¹⁴ And he has raised up for his people a horn,
   the praise of all his faithful servants,
   of Israel, the people close to his heart.

Praise the LORD.

Psalm 149

¹ Praise the LORD.

Sing to the LORD a new song,
    his praise in the assembly of his faithful people.

² Let Israel rejoice in their Maker;
    let the people of Zion be glad in their King.
³ Let them praise his name with dancing
    and make music to him with timbrel and harp.
⁴ For the LORD takes delight in his people;
    he crowns the humble with victory.
⁵ Let his faithful people rejoice in this honor
    and sing for joy on their beds.

⁶ May the praise of God be in their mouths
    and a double-edged sword in their hands,
⁷ to inflict vengeance on the nations
    and punishment on the peoples,
⁸ to bind their kings with fetters,
    their nobles with shackles of iron,
⁹ to carry out the sentence written against them—
    this is the glory of all his faithful people.

Praise the LORD.

Psalm 150

[1] Praise the LORD.

Praise God in his sanctuary;
   praise him in his mighty heavens.
[2] Praise him for his acts of power;
   praise him for his surpassing greatness.
[3] Praise him with the sounding of the trumpet,
   praise him with the harp and lyre,
[4] praise him with timbrel and dancing,
   praise him with the strings and pipe,
[5] praise him with the clash of cymbals,
   praise him with resounding cymbals.

[6] Let everything that has breath praise the LORD.

Praise the LORD.

Litanies and Akathist of Praise

The **Akathist Hymn** is a hymn recited by Eastern Catholics and Orthodox Christians. It is dedicated to one of the Persons of the Trinity, a saint or a holy event. The name derives from the fact that during the chanting of the hymn, or sometimes the whole service, the congregation is expected to remain standing in reverence, without sitting down (*a-*, "without, not" and *káthisis*, "sitting"), except for the aged or infirm.

Litany of the Praise of the Father

(Before each line say) *"Blessed are you, Father!"*

You are love itself.
You are eternal.
You are immutable.
You are holy.
You are without bounds.
You are all present.
You are all knowing.
You are all powerful.
You are the Father of our Lord Jesus.
You are the giver of the Holy Spirit.
You are the creator and sustainer of all.

You are the creator of the Seraphim.
You are the creator of the Cherubim.

You are the creator of the Thrones.
You are the creator of the Dominions.
You are the creator of the Virtues.
You are the creator of the Powers.
You are the creator of the Archangels.
You are the creator of the Principalities.
You are the creator of the Guardian Angels.

You spoke and all matter and anti-matter came to be.
You spoke and every atom came to be.
You spoke and every particle came to be.
You spoke and created every star was formed.
You spoke and every planet was formed
You spoke and every planet was formed.
You spoke and nebulae were formed.
You spoke and every black hole was formed.
You spoke and every solar system was formed.
You spoke and every galaxy was formed.
You spoke and set all things in order.

By your Word there was light.
By your Word you formed waters above the dome and
waters below the dome.
By your Word you formed the lights for the day and
the lights for the night.
By your Word you formed living creatures in the
water and every winged bird.
By your Word you formed every animal and every
creeping thing.

By your hand your hand you gave man and woman life.
By your hand you made them in your image and likeness.
By your hand you gave there frame and skin.
By your hand you gave them systems.
By your hand you gave them senses.
By your hand you gave them will.
By your hand you gave them intellect with memory
and imagination.
By your hand you made them eternal.

In your love you gave them each other.
In your love, when they fell, you promised a Redeemer.
In your love you fathered a people as your own.
In your love you sent them prophets.
In your love you sent them your Son.
In your love your Son gave his life for them.
In your love your Son rose for them.
In your love your Son gave his life to them by the Holy
Spirit.
In your love you made man and woman your sons and
daughters.
In your love we call you, "Abba!"
In your love you gathered them into a family, the
Church.
In your love your Son shall return for them.
In your love your Son will raise them from the dead.
In your love you shall wipe away their tears.
In your love you shall be their God and they shall be
your people; you eternally possessing them and
they eternally possessing you.

Blessed are you, Father! Blessed are you!

Litany of the Praise of Jesus

(Before each line say) **"I adore you, Lord Jesus!"**

You are the Second Person of the Most Holy Trinity.
You are the Word of God.
You are Co-eternal with the Father and the Spirit.
You are Consubstantial with the Father and the Spirit.
You are the Alpha and the Omega.
You are the Great I Am.
You are the Holy One of Israel.
You are the Prophesied One.
You are the Messiah, the Christ, Anointed One.
You are the Son of the Most High.
You are the Name above All Names.
You are the Bright Morning Star.
You are the Wonderful Counselor.
You are the Prince of Peace.
You are the Light of the World.
You are the Mighty Warrior.
You are the Living Water.
You are the Font of Holiness.

You are Yeshua, Yahweh who Saves.
You were incarnate in the womb of the Virgin Mary.
You are Emmanuel, God with us.
You are fully God and fully man.
You are the Son of God and the Son of Man.
You are the obedient Son of the Father.
You are humble.

You are the Healer.
You are the Teacher.
You are the Miracle Worker.
You are the One Who Cast Out Demons.
You are the Balm in Gilead.

You are the Redeemer.
You are the Good Shepherd who lays down his life for
his sheep.
You are the Bread of Life.
You are our New Covenant.
You are our Eucharistic King.
You are the Vine.
You are the Door.
You are the Sheep Gate.
You are the Way, the Truth, and the Life.
You are the Resurrection and the Life.
You are the Corner Stone rejected by the Builders.

You are Melchizedek.
You are the Servant of All.
You are the Suffering Servant.
You are our High Priest.
You are the Lamb of God who takes away the sins of
the world.
You are our Righteousness.
You are our Savior.
You are our Deliverer.
You are our Sanctification.

You are Faithful and True.
You are the Lord of Lords and the King of Kings.
You are Christ the King.

You are all that I need.
You are all that I want.
You are the Bridegroom of My Soul.
You are My Life.
You are My Love.

By your stripes we are healed.
By your blood we are saved.

I adore you, Lord Jesus! I adore you!

Litany of the Praise of the Spirit

Glory to Thee, our God, glory to Thee!

O Heavenly King, the Comforter, the Spirit of Truth, Who art everywhere and fills all things; Treasury of Blessings, and Giver of Life - come and abide in us, and cleanse us from every impurity, and save our souls, O Good One.

Holy God! Holy Mighty! Holy Immortal! Have mercy on us. (3x)

Glory to the Father, and to the Son, and to the Holy Spirit, now and ever and unto ages of ages. Amen.

(Before each line say) **"Holy Spirit, I love you!"**

You are the Third Person of the Blessed Trinity.
You are God.
You are Love.
You are the Love between the Father and the Son.
You are Co-eternal with the Father and the Son.
You are Consubstantial with the Father and the Son.
You are the Sanctifier.
You are the Power of the Most High.

You are the Spirit hovering over Creation.
You are Ruach, the Breath of God, breathed into man.

You are the Sevenfold Spirit.

You are the Spirit of Fear of the Lord.
You are the Spirit of Piety.
You are the Spirit of Counsel.
You are the Spirit of Wisdom.
You are the Spirit of Fortitude.
You are the Spirit of Knowledge.
You are the Spirit of Understanding.

You are the anointing of priests, prophets, and kings.

You descended on Jesus in the Jordan at his baptism.
You led Jesus.
You were upon Jesus with power to heal, cleanse the
leper, cast out demons, and raise the dead.
You moved through Jesus with Miracle Power.

It was through you that Jesus offered his sacrifice that
makes us whole.
You raised Jesus from the dead.

You are the Promise of the Father.
You are our Constant, Abiding, Companion.
You are our Comforter.
You are the Spirit of Sonship.
You cry out in us, "Abba, Father."

Holy Spirit, I love you!

Akathist Hymn: Glory to God for All Things
This Akathist, also called the *"Akathist of Thanksgiving,"* was found among the effects of Protopresbyter Gregory Petrov upon his death in a prison camp in 1940. The title is from the words of Saint John Chrysostom as he was dying in exile. It is a song of praise from amidst the most terrible sufferings attributed to Metropolitan Tryphon of Turkestan.

Hymn 1

Everlasting King, Thy will for our salvation is full of power. Thy right arm controls the whole course of human life. We give Thee thanks for all Thy mercies, seen and unseen. For eternal life, for the heavenly joys of the Kingdom which is to be. Grant mercy to us who sing Thy praise, both now and in the time to come. Glory to Thee, O God, from age to age.

I was born a weak, defenseless child, but Thine angel spread his wings over my cradle to defend me. From birth until now Thy love has illumined my path, and has wondrously guided me towards the light of eternity; from birth until now the generous gifts of Thy providence have been marvelously showered upon me. I give Thee thanks, with all who have come to know Thee, who call upon Thy name.

Glory to Thee for calling me into being
Glory to Thee, showing me the beauty of the universe

Glory to Thee, spreading out before me heaven and earth
Like the pages in a book of eternal wisdom
Glory to Thee for Thine eternity in this fleeting world
Glory to Thee for Thy mercies, seen and unseen
Glory to Thee through every sigh of my sorrow
Glory to Thee for every step of my life's journey
For every moment of glory
Glory to Thee, O God, from age to age

Hymn 2

O Lord, how lovely it is to be Thy guest. Breeze full of
scents; mountains reaching to the skies; waters like
boundless mirrors, reflecting the sun's golden rays and the
scudding clouds. All nature murmurs mysteriously,
breathing the depth of tenderness. Birds and beasts of the
forest bear the imprint of Thy love. Blessed art thou,
mother earth, in thy fleeting loveliness, which wakens our
yearning for happiness that will last forever, in the land
where, amid beauty that grows not old, the cry rings out:
Alleluia!

Thou hast brought me into life as into an enchanted
paradise. We have seen the sky like a chalice of deepest
blue, where in the azure heights the birds are singing. We
have listened to the soothing murmur of the forest and
the melodious music of the streams. We have tasted fruit
of fine flavor and the sweet-scented honey. We can live
very well on Thine earth. It is a pleasure to be Thy guest.
Glory to Thee for the Feast Day of life

Glory to Thee for the perfume of lilies and roses
Glory to Thee for each different taste of berry and fruit
Glory to Thee for the sparkling silver of early morning dew
Glory to Thee for the joy of dawn's awakening
Glory to Thee for the new life each day brings
Glory to Thee, O God, from age to age

Hymn 3

It is the Holy Spirit who makes us find joy in each flower, the exquisite scent, the delicate color, the beauty of the Most High in the tiniest of things. Glory and honor to the Spirit, the Giver of Life, who covers the fields with their carpet of flowers, crowns the harvest with gold, and gives to us the joy of gazing at it with our eyes. O be joyful and sing to Him: Alleluia!

How glorious art Thou in the springtime, when every creature awakes to new life and joyfully sings Thy praises with a thousand tongues. Thou art the Source of Life, the Destroyer of Death. By the light of the moon, nightingales sing, and the valleys and hills lie like wedding garments, white as snow. All the earth is Thy promised bride awaiting her spotless husband. If the grass of the field is like this, how gloriously shall we be transfigured in the Second Coming after the Resurrection! How splendid our bodies, how spotless our souls!
Glory to Thee, bringing from the depth of the earth an endless variety of *colors*, tastes and scents
Glory to Thee for the warmth and tenderness of the

world of nature

Glory to Thee for the numberless creatures around us

Glory to Thee for the depths of Thy wisdom, the whole
world a living sign of it

Glory to Thee; on my knees, I kiss the traces of Thine
unseen hand

Glory to Thee, enlightening us with the clearness of
eternal life

Glory to Thee for the hope of the unutterable,
imperishable beauty of immortality

Glory to Thee, O God, from age to age

Hymn 4

How filled with sweetness are those whose thoughts dwell
on Thee; how life-giving Thy holy Word. To speak with
Thee is more soothing than anointing with oil; sweeter
than the honeycomb. To pray to Thee lifts the spirit,
refreshes the soul. Where Thou art not, there is only
emptiness; hearts are smitten with sadness; nature, and
life itself, become sorrowful; where Thou art, the soul is
filled with abundance, and its song resounds like a torrent
of life: Alleluia!

When the sun is setting, when quietness falls like the
peace of eternal sleep, and the silence of the spent day
reigns, then in the splendor of its declining rays, filtering
through the clouds, I see Thy dwelling-place: fiery and
purple, gold and blue, they speak prophet-like of the
ineffable beauty of Thy presence, and call to us in their

majesty. We turn to the Father.

Glory to Thee at the hushed hour of nightfall

Glory to Thee, covering the earth with peace

Glory to Thee for the last ray of the sun as it sets

Glory to Thee for sleep's repose that restores us

Glory to Thee for Thy goodness even in the time of darkness

When all the world is hidden from our eyes

Glory to Thee for the prayers offered by a trembling soul

Glory to Thee for the pledge of our reawakening

On that glorious last day, that day which has no evening

Glory to Thee, O God, from age to age

Hymn 5

The dark storm clouds of life bring no terror to those in whose hearts Thy fire is burning brightly. Outside is the darkness of the whirlwind, the terror and howling of the storm, but in the heart, in the presence of Christ, there is light and peace, silence: Alleluia!

I see Thine heavens resplendent with stars. How glorious art Thou radiant with light! Eternity watches me by the rays of the distant stars. I am small, insignificant, but the Lord is at my side. Thy right arm guides me wherever I go.

Glory to Thee, ceaselessly watching over me

Glory to Thee for the encounters Thou dost arrange for me

Glory to Thee for the love of parents, for the faithfulness
of friends
Glory to Thee for the humbleness of the animals which
serve me
Glory to Thee for the unforgettable moments of life
Glory to Thee for the heart's innocent joy
Glory to Thee for the joy of living
Moving and being able to return Thy love
Glory to Thee, O God, from age to age

Hymn 6

How great and how close art Thou in the powerful track of
the storm! How mighty Thy right arm in the blinding flash
of the lightning! How awesome Thy majesty! The voice of
the Lord fills the fields; it speaks in the rustling of the
trees. The voice of the Lord is in the thunder and the
downpour. The voice of the Lord is heard above the
waters. Praise be to Thee in the roar of mountains ablaze.
Thou dost shake the earth like a garment; Thou dost pile
up to the sky the waves of the sea. Praise be to Thee,
bringing low the pride of man. Thou dost bring from his
heart a cry of Penitence: Alleluia!

When the lightning flash has lit up the camp dining hall,
how feeble seems the light from the lamp. Thus dost Thou,
like the lightning, unexpectedly light up my heart with
flashes of intense joy. After Thy blinding light, how drab,
how colorless, how illusory all else seems. My soul clings
to Thee.

Glory to Thee, the highest peak of men's dreaming
Glory to Thee for our unquenchable thirst for communion
with God
Glory to Thee, making us dissatisfied with earthly things
Glory to Thee, turning on us Thine healing rays
Glory to Thee, subduing the power of the spirits of
darkness
And dooming to death every evil
Glory to Thee for the signs of Thy presence
For the joy of hearing Thy voice and living in Thy love
Glory to Thee, O God, from age to age

Hymn 7

In the wondrous blending of sounds it is Thy call we hear;
in the harmony of many voices, in the sublime beauty of
music, in the glory of the works of great composers: Thou
leads us to the threshold of paradise to come, and to the
choirs of angels. All true beauty has the power to draw the
soul towards Thee, and to make it sing in ecstasy: Alleluia!

The breath of Thine Holy Spirit inspires artists, poets and
scientists. The power of Thy supreme knowledge makes
them prophets and interpreters of Thy laws, who reveal
the depths of Thy creative wisdom. Their works speak
unwittingly of Thee. How great art Thou in Thy creation!
How great art Thou in man!
Glory to Thee, showing Thine unsurpassable power in the
laws of the universe
Glory to Thee, for all nature is filled with Thy laws

Glory to Thee for what Thou hast revealed to us in
Thy mercy
Glory to Thee for what Thou hast hidden from us in
Thy wisdom
Glory to Thee for the inventiveness of the human mind
Glory to Thee for the dignity of man's *labor*
Glory to Thee for the tongues of fire that bring inspiration
Glory to Thee, O God, from age to age

Hymn 8

How near Thou art in the day of sickness.
Thou Thyself visits the sick; Thou Thyself bends over the
sufferer's bed. His heart speaks to Thee. In the throes of
sorrow and suffering Thou brings peace and unexpected
consolation. Thou art the comforter. Thou art the love
which watches over and heals us. To Thee we sing the
song: Alleluia!

When in childhood I called upon Thee consciously for the
first time, Thou didst hear my prayer, and Thou didst fill
my heart with the blessing of peace. At that moment I
knew Thy goodness and knew how blessed are those who
turn to Thee. I started to call upon Thee night and day; and
now even now I call upon Thy name.
Glory to Thee, satisfying my desires with good things
Glory to Thee, watching over me day and night
Glory to Thee, curing affliction and emptiness with the
healing flow of time
Glory to Thee, no loss is irreparable in Thee, Giver of

eternal life to all
Glory to Thee, making immortal all that is lofty and good
Glory to Thee, promising us the longed-for meeting with
our loved ones who have died
Glory to Thee, O God, from age to age

Hymn 9

Why is it that on a Feast Day the whole of nature
mysteriously smiles? Why is it that then a heavenly
gladness fills our hearts; a gladness far beyond that of
earth and the very air in church and in the altar becomes
luminous? It is the breath of Thy gracious love. It is the
reflection of the glory of Mount Tabor. Then do heaven
and earth sing Thy praise: Alleluia!

When Thou didst call me to serve my brothers and filled
my soul with humility, one of Thy deep, piercing rays
shone into my heart; it became luminous, full of light like
iron glowing in the furnace. I have seen Thy face, face of
mystery and of unapproachable glory.
Glory to Thee, transfiguring our lives with deeds of love
Glory to Thee, making wonderfully Sweet the keeping of
Thy commandments
Glory to Thee, making Thyself known where man shows
mercy on his *neighbor*
Glory to Thee, sending us failure and misfortune that we
may understand the sorrows of others
Glory to Thee, rewarding us so well for the good we do
Glory to Thee, welcoming the impulse of our heart's love

Glory to Thee, raising to the heights of heaven every act of love in earth and sky
Glory to Thee, O God, from age to age

Hymn 10

No one can put together what has crumbled into dust, but Thou canst restore a conscience turned to ashes. Thou canst restore to its former beauty a soul lost and without hope. With Thee, there is nothing that cannot be redeemed. Thou art love; Thou art Creator and Redeemer. We praise Thee, singing: Alleluia!

Remember, my God, the fall of Lucifer full of ride, keep me safe with the power of Thy Grace; save me from falling away from Thee. Save me from doubt. Incline my heart to hear Thy mysterious voice every moment of my life. Incline my heart to call upon Thee, present in everything.
Glory to Thee for every happening
Every condition Thy providence has put me in
Glory to Thee for what Thou *speaks* to me in my heart
Glory to Thee for what Thou reveals to me, asleep or awake
Glory to Thee for scattering our vain imaginations
Glory to Thee for raising us from the slough of our passions through suffering
Glory to Thee for curing our pride of heart by humiliation
Glory to Thee, O God, from age to age

Hymn 11

Across the cold chains of the centuries, I feel the warmth
of Thy breath; I feel Thy blood pulsing in my veins. Part of
time has already gone, but now Thou art the present. I
stand by Thy Cross; I was the cause of it. I cast myself
down in the dust before it. Here is the triumph of love, the
victory of salvation. Here the centuries themselves cannot
remain silent, singing Thy praises: Alleluia!

Blessed are they that will share in the King's Banquet: but
already on earth Thou gives me a foretaste of this
blessedness. How many times with Thine own hand hast
Thou held out to me Thy Body and Thy Blood, and I,
though a miserable sinner, have received this Mystery, and
have tasted Thy love, so ineffable, so heavenly.
Glory to Thee for the unquenchable fire of Thy Grace
Glory to Thee, building Thy Church, a haven of peace in a
tortured world
Glory to Thee for the life-giving water of Baptism in which
we find new birth
Glory to Thee, restoring to the penitent purity white as the
lily
Glory to Thee for the cup of salvation and the bread of
eternal joy
Glory to Thee for exalting us to the highest heaven
Glory to Thee, O God, from age to age

Hymn 12

How often have I seen the reflection of Thy glory in the

faces of the dead? How resplendent they were, with beauty and heavenly joy. How ethereal, how translucent their faces. How triumphant over suffering and death, their felicity and peace. Even in the silence they were calling upon Thee. In the hour of my death, enlighten my soul, too, that it may cry out to Thee: Alleluia!

What sort of praise can I give Thee? I have never heard the song of the Cherubim, a joy reserved for the spirits above. But I know the praises that nature sings to Thee. In winter, I have beheld how silently in the moonlight the whole earth offers Thee prayer, clad in its white mantle of snow, sparkling like diamonds. I have seen how the rising sun rejoices in Thee, how the song of the birds is a chorus of praise to Thee. I have heard the mysterious mutterings of the forests about Thee, and the winds singing Thy praise as they stir the waters. I have understood how the choirs of stars proclaim Thy glory as they move forever in the depths of infinite space. What is my poor worship! All nature obeys Thee, I do not. Yet while I live, I see Thy love, I long to thank Thee, and call upon Thy name.

Glory to Thee, giving us light
Glory to Thee, loving us with love so deep, divine and infinite
Glory to Thee, blessing us with light, and with the host of angels and saints
Glory to Thee, Father all-holy, promising us a share in Thy Kingdom
Glory to Thee, Redeemer Son, who hast shown us the path

to salvation!
Glory to Thee, Holy Spirit, life-giving Sun of the world to come
Glory to Thee for all things, Holy and most merciful Trinity
Glory to Thee, O God, from age to age

Hymn 13

Life-giving and merciful Trinity, receive my thanksgiving for all Thy goodness. Make us worthy of Thy blessings, so that, when we have brought to fruit the talents Thou hast entrusted to us, we may enter into the joy of our Lord, forever exulting in the shout of victory: Alleluia!

(*Repeat* Hymn 13 and Alleluia three times)

I was born a weak, defenseless child, but Thine angel spread his wings over my cradle to defend me. From birth until now Thy love has illumined my path, and has wondrously guided me towards the light of eternity; from birth until now the generous gifts of Thy providence have been marvelously showered upon me. I give Thee thanks, with all who have come to know Thee, who call upon Thy name.
Glory to Thee for calling me into being
Glory to Thee, showing me the beauty of the universe
Glory to Thee, spreading out before me heaven and earth
Like the pages in a book of eternal wisdom

Glory to Thee for Thine eternity in this fleeting world
Glory to Thee for Thy mercies, seen and unseen
Glory to Thee through every sigh of my sorrow
Glory to Thee for every step of my life's journey
For every moment of glory
Glory to Thee, O God, from age to age

Everlasting King, Thy will for our salvation is full of power.
Thy right arm controls the whole course of human life. We
give Thee thanks for all Thy mercies, seen and unseen: For
eternal life, for the heavenly Joys of the Kingdom which is
to be. Grant mercy to us who sing Thy praise, both now
and in the time to come. Glory to Thee, O God, from age to
age.

Akathist to our Sweet Lord Jesus Christ

Hymn 1

To you, Champion Leader and Lord, the Vanquisher of Hades, I, your creature and servant, offer a song of praise, for you have delivered me from eternal death. But as you have inextinguishable loving-kindness, deliver me from all dangers that can be, that I may cry to you: Jesus, Son of God, have mercy on me.

Creator of angels and Lord of hosts, as of old you opened the ear and tongue of the deaf and dumb, likewise open now my perplexed mind and tongue to the praise of your most holy name that I may cry to you:
Jesus, most wonderful, angels' astonishment!
Jesus, most powerful, forefathers' deliverance!
Jesus, most sweet, Patriarch's exultation!
Jesus, most glorious, Kings' stronghold!
Jesus, most beloved, Prophets' fulfillment!
Jesus, most marvelous, martyr's strength!
Jesus, most peaceful, monk's joy!
Jesus, most gracious, priests' sweetness!
Jesus, most merciful, fasters' abstinence!
Jesus, most tender, saints' rejoicing!
Jesus, most honorable, virgins' chastity!
Jesus, everlasting, sinners' salvation!
Jesus, Son of God, have mercy on me!

Hymn 2

As when seeing the widow weeping bitterly, O Lord, you were moved with pity, and raised her son from the dead as he was being carried to burial, likewise have pity on me, O Lover of mankind, and raise my soul, deadened by sins, as I cry:
Alleluia!

Seeking to understand the incomprehensible, Philip asked, "Lord, show us the Father," and you answered him: "Have I been so long with you and you have not yet known that I am in the Father and the Father in Me?" Likewise, O Inconceivable One, with fear I cry to you:
Jesus, Eternal God!
Jesus, All-powerful King!
Jesus, Long-suffering Master!
Jesus, All-merciful Savior!
Jesus, Gracious Guardian!
Jesus, cleanse me from my sins!
Jesus, wash me from my iniquity!
Jesus, pardon my unrighteousness!
Jesus, my Hope, do not forsake me!
Jesus, my Helper, do not reject me!
Jesus, my Creator, do not forget me!
Jesus, my Shepherd, do not destroy me!
Jesus, Son of God, have mercy on me!

Hymn 3

You who clothed your Apostles who tarried in Jerusalem with power from on high, O Jesus, clothe me also, stripped bare of all good works, with the warmth of your Holy Spirit, and grant that with love I may sing to you:
Alleluia!

In the abundance of your mercy, O Jesus, you have called publicans and sinners and infidels. Now do not despise me who am like them, but as precious myrrh, accept this song:
Jesus, invincible power!
Jesus, infinite mercy!
Jesus, radiant beauty!
Jesus, unspeakable love!
Jesus, Son of the Living God!
Jesus, have mercy on me a sinner!
Jesus, hear me who was conceived in iniquity!
Jesus, cleanse me who was born in sins!
Jesus, teach me who am worthless!
Jesus, enlighten my darkness!
Jesus, purify me who am unclean!
Jesus, restore me, a prodigal!
Jesus, Son of God, have mercy on me!

Hymn 4

Having an interior storm of doubting thoughts, Peter was sinking. But beholding you in the flesh walking on the waters, O Jesus, he confessed you to be the true God; and

receiving the hand of salvation, he cried:
Alleluia!

When the blind man heard you, O Lord, passing by on the way, he cried: "Jesus, Son of David, have mercy on me!" And you called him and opened his eyes. Likewise enlighten the spiritual eyes of my heart with Your love as I cry to You and say:
Jesus, creator of those on high
Jesus, redeemer of those below!
Jesus, vanquisher of the powers of hades!
Jesus, adorner of every creature!
Jesus, comforter of my soul!
Jesus, enlightener of my mind!
Jesus, gladness of my heart!
Jesus, health of my body!
Jesus, my Savior, save me!
Jesus, my Light, enlighten me!
Jesus, deliver me from all torments!
Jesus, save me despite my unworthiness!
Jesus, Son of God, have mercy on me!

Hymn 5

As of old You redeemed us from the curse of the law by Your Divine-flowing Blood, O Jesus, likewise rescue us from the snares in which the serpent has entangled us through the passions of the flesh, through lustful suggestions, and evil despondency, as we cry to You:
Alleluia!

Having beheld the Creator in human form and knowing Him to be the master, the Hebrew children hastened to please Him with branches, crying "Hosanna!" But we offer you a song, saying:
Jesus, True God!
Jesus, Son of David!
Jesus, most glorious King!
Jesus, blameless Lamb!
Jesus, most wonderful Shepherd!
Jesus, guardian of my infancy!
Jesus, nourisher of my youth!
Jesus, praise of my old age!
Jesus, my hope at death!
Jesus, my life after death!
Jesus, my comfort at your judgment!
Jesus, my desire, do not put me to shame!
Jesus, Son of God, have mercy on me!

Hymn 6

In fulfillment of the words and message of the God-bearing prophets, O Jesus, You appeared on earth, and You who are uncontainable dwelt with men, and took our infirmities; being healed by your wounds, we have learned to sing:
Alleluia!

The light of Your Truth shone upon the world, and demonic delusion was driven away; for the idols have fallen, O our Savior, unable to endure Your strength. But we, having received salvation, cry to You:

Jesus, the Truth, dispelling falsehood!
Jesus, the Light, above all radiance!
Jesus, the King, surpassing all in strength!
Jesus, God, constant in mercy!
Jesus, Bread of Life, fill me who am hungry!
Jesus, Source of knowledge, give me drink who am thirsty!
Jesus, Garment of gladness, clothe me the corruptible!
Jesus, Shelter of joy, cover me, the unworthy!
Jesus, Giver to those that ask, give me sorrow for my sins!
Jesus, Finder of those that seek, find my soul!
Jesus, Opener to those that knock, open my wretched heart!
Jesus, Redeemer of sinners, blot out my transgressions!
Jesus, Son of God, have mercy on me!

Hymn 7

Desiring to reveal the mystery hidden from the ages, you were led as a sheep to the slaughter, O Jesus, and as a lamb before its shearer. But as God You rose from the dead and ascended with glory to heaven, and along with Yourself You raised us who cry:
Alleluia!

The creator has shown us a marvelous Creature, who was incarnate of a virgin without seed, rose from the tomb without breaking the seal, and entered bodily the Apostles' room when the doors were shut. Wherefore,

marveling at this, we sing:
Jesus, infinite word!
Jesus, inscrutable word!
Jesus, incomprehensible power!
Jesus, inconceivable wisdom!
Jesus, inexpressible divinity!
Jesus, boundless dominion!
Jesus, invincible kingdom!
Jesus, endless sovereignty!
Jesus, supreme strength!
Jesus, power eternal!
Jesus, my Creator, have compassion on me!
Jesus, my Savior, save me!
Jesus, Son of God, have mercy on me!

Hymn 8

Seeing God wondrously incarnate, let us shun the vain
world and set our mind on things divine; for God came
down to earth that He might raise to heaven us who cry to
Him:
Alleluia!

The immeasurable One was below all things, yet in no way
separated from things above, when He willingly suffered
for our sake, and by
His death our death was put to death, and by His
resurrection granted life to those who sing:
Jesus, heart's sweetness!
Jesus, body's strength!

Jesus, soul's radiance!
Jesus, mind's swiftness!
Jesus, conscience's joy!
Jesus, well known hope!
Jesus, memory before the ages!
Jesus, high praise!
Jesus, my supremely exalted glory!
Jesus, my desire, do not reject me!
Jesus, my shepherd, seek me!
Jesus, my Savior, save me!
Jesus, Son of God, have mercy on me!

Hymn 9

All the angelic nature of heaven glorifies unceasingly your most Holy Name, O Jesus, crying "Holy, holy, holy!" But we sinners on earth with lips of dust cry:
Alleluia!

We see the most eloquent orators voiceless as fish concerning You, O Jesus our Savior; for they are at a loss to say how you are perfect man, yet remain God immutable; but we, marveling at this mystery, cry faithfully:
Jesus, God before the ages!
Jesus, King of kings!
Jesus, Master of rulers!
Jesus, Judge of the living and the dead!
Jesus, Hope of the hopeless!
Jesus, Comfort of those who mourn!
Jesus, Glory of the poor!

Jesus, do not condemn me because of my deeds!
Jesus, cleanse me according to Your mercy!
Jesus, drive from me despondency!
Jesus, enlighten the thoughts of my heart!
Jesus, grant me to remember my death!
Jesus, Son of God, have mercy on me!

Hymn 10

Desiring to save the world, O Sunrise of the East, You took upon yourself the sinister direction of our nature, and humbled Yourself even unto death; thus, your name is supremely exalted above every name, and from all the tribes of heaven and earth You hear: Alleluia!

Eternal King, Comforter, true Christ! Cleanse us of every stain, as you cleansed the ten lepers; and heal us, as You healed the greedy soul of Zacchaeus the Publican, that we may shout to You with compunction, crying aloud:
Jesus, treasury incorruptible!
Jesus, wealth unfailing!
Jesus, strong food!
Jesus, drink inexhaustible!
Jesus, garment of the poor!
Jesus, protection of widows!
Jesus, defender of orphans!
Jesus, help of toilers!
Jesus, guide of pilgrims!
Jesus, pilot of voyagers!
Jesus, calmer of tempests!

Jesus, God, raise me who am fallen!
Jesus, Son of God, have mercy on me!

Hymn 11

Though unworthy, I offer you tender songs, and like the woman of Canaan, I cry to You: "O Jesus, have mercy on me!" For it is not a daughter, but my flesh that is cruelly possessed with passions and burning with fury. So grant healing to me, who cry to You:
Alleluia!

Having previously persecuted You, the Light-bestowing Lamp of those in the darkness of ignorance, Paul heeded the power of the voice of Divine enlightenment, and understood the swiftness of the soul's conversion; lighten also the light of my dark soul as I cry:
Jesus, my most mighty King!
Jesus, my most powerful God!
Jesus, my immortal Lord!
Jesus, my most glorious Creator!
Jesus, my most good Guide!
Jesus, my most compassionate Shepherd!
Jesus, my most merciful Master!
Jesus, my most gracious Savior!
Jesus, enlighten my senses darkened by passions!
Jesus, heal my body scabbed with sins!
Jesus, cleanse my mind of vain thoughts!
Jesus, keep my heart from evil desires!
Jesus, Son of God, have mercy on me!

Hymn 12

Grant me Your grace, O Jesus, Absolver of all debts, and receive me who am repenting, as you received Peter who denied You, and call me who am downcast, as of old You called Paul who persecuted You, and hear me as I cry to You.

Alleluia!

Praising Your incarnation, we all extol You, and we believe with Thomas that You are Lord and God, sitting with the Father and coming to judge the living and the dead. Grant me then to stand on Your right hand, who now cry:

Jesus, King before the ages, have mercy on me!

Jesus, sweet scented flower, make me fragrant!

Jesus, beloved warmth, make me fervent!

Jesus, eternal temple, shelter me!

Jesus, garment of light, adorn me!

Jesus, pearl of great price, enlighten me!

Jesus, precious stone, illumine me!

Jesus, sun of righteousness, shine on me!

Jesus, Holy light, make me radiant!

Jesus, from sickness of soul and body deliver me!

Jesus, from the hands of the adversary, rescue me!

Jesus, from the unquenchable fire and other eternal torments save me!

Jesus, Son of God, have mercy on me!

Hymn 13

O most sweet and all-compassionate Jesus! Receive now this our small supplication, as You received the widow's two mites, and keep Your inheritance from all enemies, visible and invisible, from foreign invasion, from disease and famine, from all tribulations and mortal wounds, and rescue from the torment to come all that cry to You:
Alleluia!
Alleluia!
Alleluia!

Creator of angels and Lord of hosts, as of old you opened the ear and tongue of the deaf and dumb, likewise open now my perplexed mind and tongue to the praise of your most holy name that I may cry to you:
Jesus, most wonderful, angels' astonishment!
Jesus, most powerful, forefathers' deliverance!
Jesus, most sweet, Patriarch's exultation!
Jesus, most glorious, Kings' stronghold!
Jesus, most beloved, Prophets' fulfillment!
Jesus, most marvelous, martyr's strength!
Jesus, most peaceful, monk's joy!
Jesus, most gracious, priests' sweetness!
Jesus, most merciful, fasters' abstinence!
Jesus, most tender, saints' rejoicing!
Jesus, most honorable, virgins' chastity!
Jesus, everlasting, sinners' salvation!
Jesus, Son of God, have mercy on me!

To you, Champion Leader and Lord, the Vanquisher of Hades, I, your creature and servant, offer a song of praise, for you have delivered me from eternal death. But as you have inextinguishable loving-kindness, deliver me from all dangers that can be, that I may cry to you: Jesus, Son of God, have mercy on me!

To you, O Lord, the only good one who does not remember evils, I confess my sins, I fall down before you, unworthy as I am, crying out: "I have sinned, O Lord, I have sinned, and I am not worthy to look upon the height of heaven for the multitude of my iniquities." But, my Lord, O Lord, grant me tears of compunction, you who alone are good and merciful, so that with them I may beg of you to cleanse me of all sin before the end; for frightful and terrible is the place that I must pass through when I have separated from this body, and a multitude of dark and inhuman demons awaits me, and there is no one to come to my help or deliver me; wherefore, I fall down before your goodness: Do not deliver me up to those who wrong me, nor let my enemies triumph over me, O Good Lord, nor let them say: you have come into our hands and you have been delivered to us. Neither, O Lord, forget your compassions, and do not render to me as my iniquities deserve, and do not turn your countenance away from me; but, O Lord, chasten me, with mercy and compassion, and do not let my enemy rejoice over me, and bring to nothingness all his deeds. And grant me an unsullied way to you, O Good Lord, because, having sinned, I have not had recourse to any other physician, and have not stretched out my hands to a strange god. Therefore, do not reject my supplication, but hearken to me in your goodness, and strengthen my heart in your fear; and let your grace be on me, O Lord, like a fire consuming the impure thoughts within me. For You, O Lord, are the Light above all lights, the Joy above all joy, the Repose above all repose, the True Life, and the Salvation that abides to the ages of ages.

AMEN.

Prayers of Praise

Divine Praises

Blessed be God.
Blessed be His Holy Name.
Blessed be Jesus Christ, true God and true Man. Blessed be
the Name of Jesus.
Blessed be His Most Sacred Heart.
Blessed be Jesus in the Most Holy Sacrament of the Altar.
Blessed be the great Mother of God, Mary most holy.
Blessed be her holy and Immaculate Conception. Blessed
be the name of Mary, Virgin and Mother. Blessed be Saint
Joseph, her most chaste Spouse. Blessed be God in His
Angels and in His Saints.

O Jesus, King Most Wonderful

O Jesus, King most wonderful! Thou Conqueror renowned!
Thou Sweetness most ineffable! In whom all joys are
found! When once Thou visits the heart, then truth begins
to shine; then earthly vanities depart; then kindles love
divine. O Jesu! Light of all below! Thou Fount of life and
fire! Surpassing all the joys we know, and all we can desire.
May every heart confess Thy name, and ever Thee adore;
And seeking Thee, itself inflame to see Thee more and
more. Thee may our tongues forever bless; Thee may we
love alone; And ever in our lives express the image of
Thine own. Amen.

Jesus, the Very Thought of Thee

Jesus, the very thought of Thee with sweetness fills the breast! Yet sweeter far Thy face to see and in Thy presence rest. No voice can sing, no heart can frame, nor can the memory find, a sweeter sound than Jesus' name, the Savior of mankind. O hope of every contrite heart! O joy of all the meek! To those who fall, how kind Thou art! How good to those who seek! But what to those who find? Ah! This nor tongue nor pen can show - The love of Jesus, what it is, none but His loved ones know. Jesus! Our only hope be Thou, as Thou our prize shalt be, in Thee be all our glory now, and through eternity. Amen.

St Francis of Assisi Canticle of Creation

Most High, all-powerful, good Lord,
Yours are the praises, the glory, the honor, and all blessing.
To You alone, Most High, do they belong, and no man is worthy to mention Your name.
Praised be You, my Lord, with all your creatures, especially Sir Brother Sun, Who brings the day and through whom You give us light. And he is beautiful and radiant with great splendor; and bears a likeness of You, Most High One.
Praised be You, my Lord, through Sister Moon and the stars, in heaven You formed them clear and precious and beautiful.
Praised be You, my Lord, through Brother Wind, and

through the air, cloudy and serene, and every kind of weather through which You give sustenance to Your creatures.

Praised be You, my Lord, through Sister Water, which is very useful and humble and precious and chaste. Praised be You, my Lord, through Brother Fire, through whom You light the night and he is beautiful and playful and robust and strong.

Praised be You, my Lord, through our Sister Mother Earth, who sustains and governs us, and who produces varied fruits with colored flowers and herbs.

Praised be You, my Lord, through those who give pardon for love of You and bear infirmity and tribulation. Blessed are those who endure in peace for by You, Most High, they shall be crowned.

Praised be You, my Lord, through our Sister Bodily Death, from whom no living man can escape. Woe to those who die in mortal sin! Blessed are those whom death will find in Your most holy will, for the second death shall do them no harm.

Praise and bless my Lord and give Him thanks and serve Him with great humility.

Ancient Prayer of Thanksgiving

We thank you, holy Father, for your holy name, which you have caused to dwell in our hearts; and for the knowledge and faith and immortality which you have made known to us through Jesus your Son. Glory be to you forever. You, almighty Master, have created all things for your name's sake, and have given food and drink to men for their enjoyment, so that they might return thanks to you. Upon us, however, you have bestowed spiritual food and drink, and eternal life through your Servant. Above all we give you thanks, because you are mighty. Glory be to you forever. Remember, O Lord, your Church. Deliver it from every evil and perfect it in your love. Gather it from the four winds, sanctified for your kingdom, which you have prepared for it. For yours is the power and the glory forever. Let grace come, and let this world pass away. Hosanna to the God of David. If anyone is holy, let him come; if anyone is not, let him repent. Maranatha. Amen. (Didache, c. 140 A.D.)

Te Deum

O, God, we praise You and acknowledge You to be the supreme Lord.
Everlasting Father, all the earth worships You.
All the angels, the heavens and all angelic powers,
All the cherubim and seraphim, continually cry to you:
Holy, holy, holy, Lord God of Hosts!

Heaven and earth are full of the majesty of Your glory.
The glorious choir of the apostles,
The wonderful company of prophets,
The white-robed army of martyrs, praise You.
Holy Church throughout the world acknowledges You:
The Father of infinite majesty;

Your adorable, true and only Son;
Also the Holy Spirit, the Comforter.
O Christ, You are the King of glory!
You are the everlasting Son of the Father.
When You took it upon Yourself to deliver man,
You did not disdain the Virgin's womb.
Having overcome the sting of death,
You opened the kingdom of heaven to all believers.
You sit at the right hand of God in the glory of the Father
We believe that You will come to be our Judge.
We, therefore, beg You to help Your servants
whom You have redeemed with Your Precious Blood.
Let them be numbered with Your saints in everlasting
glory.

Litany of Being Wonderfully Made

Abba, my Father,
I rejoice and give you thanks, for I am fearfully and wonderfully made - body, soul, and spirit. You have knit me together in your image and desire to conform me to your likeness. Abba, my Father, I rejoice in the gift of my spirit which enables me to come into communion with you and receive your revelation.

I am fearfully and wonderfully made.

Abba, my Father, I rejoice in my soul with its will, intellect, and emotions.

I am fearfully and wonderfully made.

Abba, my Father, I rejoice in my body with its systems and senses.

I am fearfully and wonderfully made.

Blessed are you, Elohim, my Father-Creator,
for my integument and exocrine Systems.

I give you thanks!

Blessed are you, Elohim, my Father-Creator,
for my skeletal and muscular systems.

I give you thanks!

Blessed are you, Elohim, my Father-Creator,
for my nervous system.

I give you thanks!

Blessed are you, Elohim, my Father-Creator,
for my endocrine system.

I give you thanks!

Blessed are you, Elohim, my Father-Creator,
for my cardiovascular and circulatory systems.

I give you thanks!

Blessed are you, Elohim, my Father-Creator,
for my respiratory systems.
I give you thanks!
Blessed are you, Elohim, my Father-Creator,
for my digestive and excretory systems.
I give you thanks!
Blessed are you, Elohim, my Father-Creator,
for my renal and urinary systems.
I give you thanks!
Blessed are you, Elohim, my Father-Creator,
for my lymphatic and immune system.
I give you thanks!
Blessed are you, Elohim, my Father-Creator,
for my reproductive system
I give you thanks!
Above all, for your great love for me in giving your Son,
Jesus, Lover of Mankind, to die and rise that I might share
life with you for all eternity,
I give you thanks!

I rejoice in every moment of my life, whether it be a time
of rejoicing or a time of difficulty. My life is precious to you
and you have danced over my life at every moment.

For the gift of my mother and my father,
I say, "I am blessed!"
For the moment of my conception,
I say, "I am blessed!"
As you knit me together and caused the genetic
combination that makes me to be the person I am,
I say, "I am blessed!"
For the moment of my birth,

I say, "I am blessed!"
As time passed and my thoughts and ideas were able to form,
I say, "I am blessed!"
For relationships in which I was loved with your love,
I say, "I am blessed!"
For the relationships in which I was not loved,
I say, "I am blessed!"
For the love of family and friends which has shaped me into who I am,
I say, "I am blessed!"
For the struggles which have come through enemies and have invited me to love,
I say, "I am blessed!"
For all that I have created,
I say, "I am blessed!"
For all that I have learned,
I say, "I am blessed!"
For all that I remember and do not remember,
I say, "I am blessed!"
For all of my past, for all of my present, and for all of my future,
I say, "I am blessed!"
For the dream you dreamed and I have become, by your grace,
I say, "I am blessed!"
For the day of my last breathing in and breathing out,
I say, "I am blessed!"
For the day when I will stand before you in the judgement of perfect love,
I say, "I am blessed!"
In hopes that I will always accept the gift of your love and

spend forever receiving your love and returning that love
back to you,

        I say, "I am blessed!"

For all that I am and will be,

        I say, "I am blessed!"

Abba, my Father,
by your hand I am fearfully and wonderfully made. May I
never take for granted the gift of my life which you have
given me. Take my life and do with it as you will. I offer
you all that I am to be used for your glory and honor.
Through, with, and in Jesus, by the power of the Holy
Spirit, may all glory and honor be yours for ages unto ages.
AMEN.

More books from City of the Lord

To all who seek to be faithful to God.

As God commanded the Israelites when He gave His Commandments to Moses, "Remember to keep holy the Sabbath." Both Jews and Christians have learned the wisdom of being faithful to this command in the context of the culture in which we live today.

While far too many Christians proclaim they are "too busy" to worship God each Sunday, there are other sincere people of faith who struggle to understand this Commandment beyond the simple obligation to attend Mass.

In his book *Keeping Holy the Lord's Day* Gabriel Meyer provides a profound reflection on the meaning of this Commandment and how a person's life and that of family and community will be enriched if people rediscover and recommit themselves to keeping the Lord's Day holy. While Mr. Meyer presents this material in a manner that is especially suitable for reflection by Catholics. Any person of faith will benefit from reading this work and thinking about how the principles that are expressed can find suitable application in their lives. Rather than being overcome by the pressures of our contemporary culture with its pressing demands, I commend this book to your reading and trust that you will find it both helpful and challenging as you seek to be faithful to God's command to "keep holy the Sabbath."

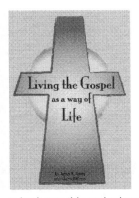

Today's secular media tends to label Catholic culture as a throwback, an anachronism in the modern world, out of step and out of touch. Whether you are single or married, with children or without, consecrated or laity, new to the faith or a long-time parishioner, *Living the Gospel as a Way of Life* will show you how building a Catholic culture is both possible and relevant for today. This marvelous, timely book provides practical wisdom for those who yearn to build or rebuild a Catholic, Christian culture in their homes, religious orders, or parishes.

Living the Gospel as a Way of Life leads one to reflect seriously on the very personal call to live as a disciple of Jesus and to do so within a relationship with others. At the heart of this book is the positive challenge to live the Gospel as a way of life. We are called to reflect on the question, what is the proper orientation of a person's life if we are focused rightly on loving God first, by living in relationship with others? While honestly facing the truth that life takes a toll on all of us, when we have learned in a positive way to live a "repentant life," we walk in the footsteps of Moses, the Prophets, John the Baptist and Jesus Christ. In this book you will find helpful principles for developing a spiritual culture in your home and wherever you find yourself, whether with one person or within the context of community life

www.cityofthelord.org

40237703R00060

Made in the USA
San Bernardino, CA
15 October 2016